TOO MANY MONKEYS!

A COUNTING RHYME

ILLUSTRATED BY KELLY OECHSLI

Golden Press • New York
Western Publishing Company, Inc.
Racine, Wisconsin

GHIJ

1
ONE

One little monkey
Wondering what to do.
Another monkey joins him.
Now there are . . .

2
TWO

Two little monkeys
Climbing up a tree!
One monkey joins them.
Now there are . . .

3
THREE

Three little monkeys
Knocking at the door!
One monkey joins them.
Now there are . . .

4
FOUR

Four little monkeys
About to take a dive!
One monkey joins them.
Now there are . . .

TICK-TOCK
TICK-TOCK
TICK-TOCK

5
FIVE

Five little monkeys
Looking for the ticks!
One monkey joins them.
Now there are . . .

6
SIX

Six little monkeys—
The bravest one is Kevin!
One monkey joins them.
Now there are . . .

7
SEVEN

Seven little monkeys—
Down the hill they skate!
One monkey joins them.
Now there are . . .

8
EIGHT

Eight little monkeys
Climbing up a vine!
One monkey joins them.
Now there are . . .

9
NINE

Nine little monkeys
Swinging high, and then,
One monkey joins them.
And that makes . . .

10
TEN

Too many monkeys!
They all fall on the ground.
Ten laughing monkeys,
What a funny sound!

10
TEN

Ten little monkeys
Sitting down to dine!
One monkey leaves them.
Now there are . . .

9

NINE

Nine little monkeys
All but one feel great!
That monkey leaves them.
Now there are . . .

8
EIGHT

Eight little monkeys—
The strongest one is Kevin!
One monkey leaves them.
Now there are . . .

7
SEVEN

Seven little monkeys
Up to brand-new tricks!
One monkey leaves them.
Now there are . . .

6
SIX

Six little monkeys
Eating honey from a hive!
One monkey leaves them.
Now there are . . .

5
FIVE

Five little monkeys
Racing to the shore!
One monkey leaves them.
Now there are . . .

4
FOUR

Four little monkeys
Sailing on the sea!
One monkey leaves them.
Now there are . . .

3
THREE

Three little monkeys—
What a sorry crew!
One monkey leaves them.
Now there are . . .

2
TWO

Two little monkeys
Still on the run!
One monkey leaves and
Now there is . . .